50 words about
Insects

David and Patricia Armentrout

Rourke
Publishing LLC
Vero Beach, Florida 32964

www.rourkepublishing.com

PHOTO CREDITS: © James P. Rowan pages 6 top, 8 top, 9 top, 10 top, 11, 12 bottom, 18 top, 19 top, 21 top, 22 bottom, 23, 24 bottom, 25; © Armentrout pages 7 bottom, 15 bottom, 16 top, 20 top, 27 bottom; © Painet, Inc. pages 12 top, 16 bottom; © PhotoDisc pages 7 top, 8 bottom, 9 bottom, 15 top, 20 bottom, 22 top, 24 top; © Brand X Pictures all other photos

Editor: Frank Sloan

Cover and page design by Nicola Stratford

Library of Congress Cataloging-in-Publication Data

Armentrout, David, 1962-
  Insects / David and Patricia Armentrout.
      p. cm. — (50 words about)
Summary: Provides simple definitions for fifty words related to insects
along with sample sentences using each word.
  ISBN 1-58952-344-X (hardcover)
  1. Insects—Juvenile literature. [1. Insects—Dictionaries.] I.
Armentrout, Patricia, 1960- II. Title.

  QL467.2 .A73 2002
  595.7—dc21

                                                        2002002376

Printed in the USA

CG/CG

insect (IN sekt)

A small animal with six legs, three main body parts, and an outer skeleton. An insect has no backbone and may have one or two pairs of wings.

abdomen

The back part of an insect.

The abdomen can be seen just behind the wings.

abdomen

adult

Fully grown.

A butterfly goes through three growth stages on the way to becoming an adult.

ant

A tiny insect that lives in a colony.

Every ant in the colony has a special job.

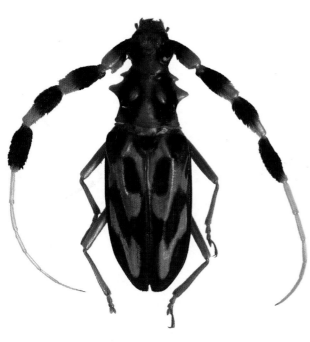

antennae

Feelers on the head of an insect used to sense its surroundings.

Insects use their antennae to find their way in the dark.

aphid

A tiny insect that sucks juice from plants.

Many kinds of ants drink a liquid called honeydew that is made in the body of aphid insects.

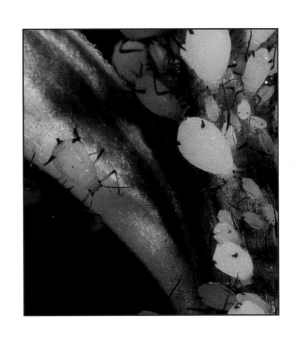

arthropod

The class, or group of animals, in which insects are placed.

Arthropods come in many shapes, colors, and sizes.

bee

A flying insect with a stinger.

Bees feed on the pollen found in flowers.

beetle

An insect with hard wings that cover and protect a pair of soft wings.

There are more kinds of beetles than any other animal.

bug

An insect with mouthparts that pierce and suck.

The stinkbug is a bug known for its strong odor.

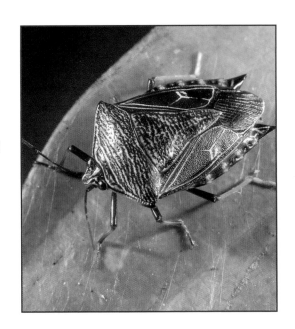

butterfly

An insect with large, often colorful wings.

A butterfly finds food and a place to rest on a flower.

camouflage

A color or cover that makes an animal look like its surroundings.

Some insects use camouflage to confuse hungry predators.

caterpillar

A growth stage of a butterfly or moth; the larva of a butterfly or moth.

A caterpillar looks nothing like the butterfly it will become.

chrysalis

A growth stage of a butterfly or moth; the pupa of a butterfly or moth.

The adult butterfly will soon emerge from a chrysalis.

cocoon

A silk case made by insects to protect themselves or their eggs.

A cocoon is made of silk spun by some insect larvae.

colony

A group of insects, or other animals, that live together.

More than one million termites can live in a single colony.

compound eye

An eye made up of many smaller eyes.

In the animal kingdom, only arthropods have compound eyes.

egg

A shell that protects baby animals before they hatch.

Insects may lay thousands of eggs.

entomology

The scientific study of insects.

A scientist who studies entomology is called an entomologist.

exoskeleton

A hard outside shell or outer skeleton.

A beetle's exoskeleton can be very colorful.

female

The sex of an animal that gives birth or lays eggs.

Not all ladybugs are female.

fly

An insect with two wings.

There are many kinds of flies, but the housefly is the most well-known.

grasshopper

A leaping, plant-eating insect.

A grasshopper's long legs make it a champion jumper.

habitat

The place where an animal lives.

A wildflower field makes a great insect habitat.

head

The front part of an insect which has antennae, eyes, and mouthparts.

Close up, an ant's head looks like a monster.

honey

A sweet, sticky substance made by bees.

Honey makes a biscuit worth eating.

honeycomb

A huge group of six-sided wax cells built by honeybees.

A honeycomb may contain thousands of wax cells.

invertebrate

An animal with no backbone.

All insects are invertebrates.

jaws

Movable mouthparts.

Most insects have more than one set of jaws.

larva

An animal that looks nothing like its parents; a caterpillar, maggot, or grub.

Ant larvae are also known as grubs.

legs

The parts of an insect used for walking or jumping.

An insect has three pairs of legs.

life cycle

The changes each living thing goes through from birth to death.

Molting is one stage of the life cycle that some insects go through.

male

The sex of an animal that can father young.

The male praying mantis is often killed by the female after mating.

mandibles

Jaws that pierce.

Mandibles may be used for biting, chewing, or defense.

migrate

To travel to another place the same time every year.

Monarch butterflies migrate between Mexico and the United States.

molt

To shed the outer layer of the body.

A cicada molts from its nymph stage to adult.

moth

Moths are similar to butterflies.

Most moths fly at night and have furry antennae.

nectar

A sweet juice from a plant.

Butterflies and other insects feed on flower nectar.

nest

A place built by animals to lay eggs or raise young.

Paper wasps mix paper fibers from dry wood and bark with their own saliva to make a nest.

nymph

Young insects that look like their parents.

This cicada nymph will soon molt into an adult.

pests

Insects that destroy crops and garden plants.

Pests feed on leaves, often killing the plant.

pollinate

To carry pollen to the female part of a plant.

Bees pollinate plants by picking up pollen from one plant and carrying it to another.

predator

An animal that hunts other animals for food.

An ambush bug is an insect predator.

prey

An animal that is hunted by another animal for food.

A crab spider catches its prey—a plume moth.

pupa

The third stage of growth of some insects.

This pupa will soon change into a moth.

sense

A power an animal uses to learn about its surroundings.

A hairy red ant uses its fine hair as a sense organ to feel movement.

species

One certain kind of animal.

A hissing cockroach is one species of cockroach.

spider

Not an insect, but a small creature with two body parts, eight legs, and no wings.

There are more than 30,000 kinds of spiders.

stinger

A pointed organ, also called a sting, used to inject venom, or poison.

The stinger is located at the rear of some insects.

thorax

The middle part of an insect where the legs are attached.

In flying insects, the wings are also attached to the thorax.

wings

A pair of light, movable body parts that enable an insect to fly.

Not all insects have wings. However, some have two pair.

Pronunciation Key

abdomen (AB duh men)
adult (uh DULHT)
ant (ANT)
antennae (an TEN uh)
aphid (AY fid)
arthropod (AR thruh pahd)
bee (BEE)
beetle (BEE tuhl)
bug (BUHG)
butterfly (BUHT er fly)
camouflage (KAM uh flahzh)
caterpillar (KAT er pil er)
chrysalis (KRIS eh les)
cocoon (kuh KOON)
colony (KOL uh nee)
compound eye (KOM pound I)
egg (EG)
entomology
  (ent uh MAHL eh jee)
exoskeleton
  (eks oh SKEL et en)
female (FEE mayl)
fly (FLY)
grasshopper (GRASS hop er)
habitat (HAB uh tat)
head (HED)
honey (HUHN ee)

honeycomb
  (HUHN ee kohm)
invertebrate
  (IN VERT e bret)
jaws (JAWZ)
larva (LAR vuh)
legs (LEGZ)
life cycle (LYF CY kul)
male (MAYL)
mandibles (MAN de bulz)
migrate (MY grayt)
molt (MOHLT)
moth (MAWTH)
nectar (NEK ter)
nest (NEST)
nymph (NIMF)
pests (PESTS)
pollinate (POL uh nayt)
predator (PRED uh ter)
prey (PRAY)
pupa (PYOO puh)
sense (SENS)
species (SPEE sheez)
spider (SPY der)
stinger (STING er)
thorax (THOR aks)
wings (WINGZ)

29

Did you know

...insects live on land, fresh water, salt water, and in polar regions? The greatest number of insects live in warm tropical areas.

Did you know

...over 800,000 kinds of insects have been named? Scientists believe there are still hundreds of thousands yet to be discovered.

Did you know

...the largest living insects (a type of stick insect) are almost a foot long (30.48 centimeters)?

Did you know

...a one gallon jar can hold 72-80 thousand ladybugs?

Did you know

...some ants can carry up to 50 times their own weight?

Did you know

...it takes up to 17 years for some cicadas to mature? The common housefly matures in 10 days.

Index

Further Reading

Mound, Laurence. *Eyewitness Books Insect,*
  Alfred A. Knopf, Inc., 1990.
Reader's Digest Pathfinders Insects and Spiders,
  Reader's Digest Children's Books Inc., 2000

Websites to Visit

www.enchantedlearning.com
www.pbs.org
www.nationalgeographic.org

About the Authors

David and Patricia Armentrout specialize in nonfiction writing.
They have had several books published for primary school
reading. They reside in Cincinnati, Ohio, with their two children.